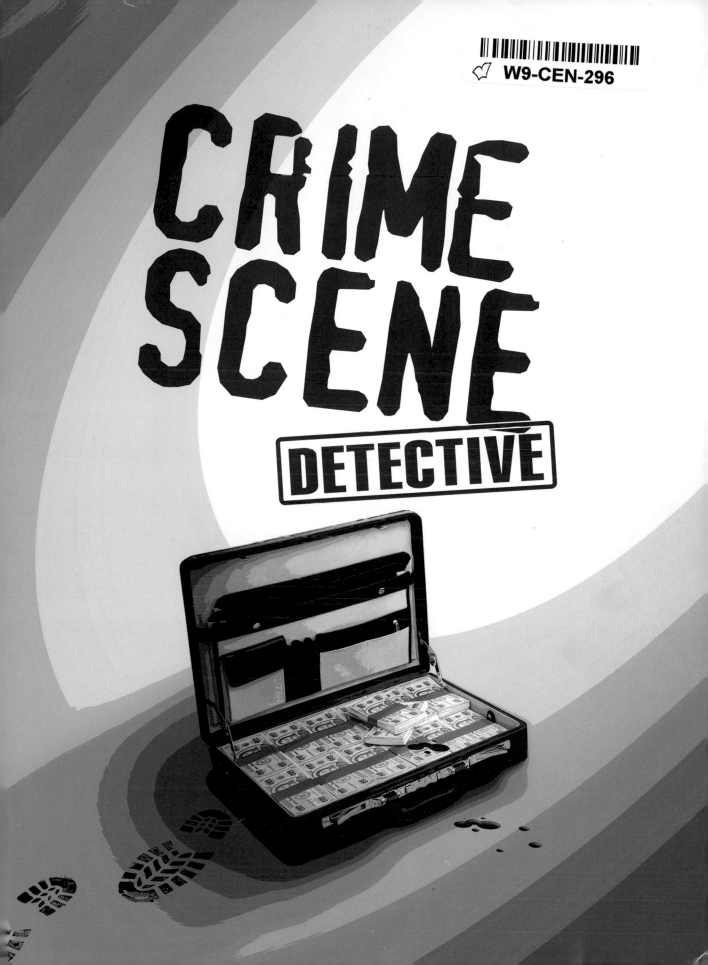

CRIME SCENE

DETECTIVE

CRIME SCENE CRIME SCENE CRIME

CRIME SCENE

DETECTIVE

Become a forensics super sleuth, with do-it-yourself activities

SCENE CRIME SCENE CRIME SCENE

Carey Scott

DK

LONDON, NEW YORK,
MELBOURNE, MUNICH, AND DELHI

Editor Jenny Finch
Designer Spencer Holbrook
Senior Editors Francesca Baines, Claire Nottage
Senior Art Editor Stefan Podhorodecki
Managing Editor Linda Esposito
Managing Art Editor Diane Thistlethwaite
Design Development Manager Sophia M. Tampakopolous Turner
Publishing Manager Andrew Macintyre
Category Publisher Laura Buller
Picture Researcher Liz Moore
DK Picture Library Claire Bowers
Production Controller Claire Pearson
DTP Designer Siu Chan
Jacket Editor Mariza O'Keeffe
Jacket Designer Yumiko Tahata
US Editor Margaret Parrish
Photography Dave King
Consultants Peter Whent, Jonathan Wright

First published in hardback in the United States in 2007
This paperback edition first published in 2009
by DK Publishing
375 Hudson Street
New York, New York 10014

09 10 11 10 (PB) 9 8 7 6 5 4 3 2 1
CD170 – 03/09

Paperback edition ISBN: 978-0-75665-155-8

Printed and bound by Leo Paper Products Ltd., China

Discover more at
www.dk.com

CONTENTS

BE SAFE! IMPORTANT NOTE TO PARENTS
Some of the activities in this book require adult
supervision. Symbols are used to indicate where an activity
must only be done with the help of an adult. Please
check carefully which activities require adult supervision
and supervise your child where indicated.

⚠ Take extra care when doing this activity.

 Activities shown with this symbol must only be done
with the help of an adult.

Always ensure that your child follows instructions carefully.
The author and the publisher cannot take responsibility for
any accident or injury that occurs because the reader has
not followed the instructions properly and will not be
responsible for any loss or damage allegedly arising from
any of the activities in this book.

CHILDREN—BE SAFE!
READ THIS BEFORE STARTING ANY ACTIVITIES!
1. Tell an adult before you do any of the activities in this
   book as you may need an adult to supervise the activity.
2. Pay attention to the following symbols:

⚠ Take extra care with an activity.

👥 You need an adult to help you with an activity.

3. Follow the instructions carefully.

THE DETECTIVE WORK

In a criminal investigation, a team of crime scene investigators (CSIs) gather evidence at the crime scene. But it is the detective in charge who directs the inquiry, drawing on knowledge and intuition for the task. In this book, you will be the detective. You'll pick up the knowledge you need as you read. So, trust your intuition and get ready to be a detective!

In court
Forensic science means science intended for a court of law. In court, forensic evidence is presented alongside conventional evidence, such as witness statements, to try to establish proof beyond a reasonable doubt.

Searching for clues
The first task is to search for any evidence and information at the crime scene.

Locard's exchange principle
In the early 1900s, Frenchman Edmund Locard formulated a theory that underpins forensic science to this day: "every contact leaves a trace." A criminal always leaves traces at a scene and takes traces of the scene away.

Be the detective...
...can you solve the four crimes?

Enter the crime scene

Take a look around and read the analysis to find out what has happened. By the time you arrive at the crime scene, CSIs have identified and isolated the items they want forensic experts to examine.

INTERESTING CLUES are discussed in more detail

ACTIVITIES let you try out the forensics for yourself

Check out the forensics

After studying the crime scene, read on to find out about the relevant areas of forensic science. Case analysis boxes keep you posted on the investigation, and activities along the way will help you to understand the science. After this, you'll be ready to crack the case.

CASE ANALYSIS boxes keep you updated on forensic tests relevant to the crime

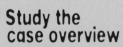

Study the case overview

Here you'll find the results of the investigation. Start by reading the police reports on the various suspects. The answer to the crime is in the forensic reports, but it'll take all your detective skills to work it out. You can check your answer on pages 70–1.

THE CRIME SCENE

The wail of police sirens pierces the airwaves, a crowd of bystanders surrounds the area, and the scene is crawling with uniformed officers. A crime scene does not remain as the criminals left it for long. In order to minimize disturbance to the crime scene and preserve fragile evidence, it is vital that CSIs follow crime-scene procedure in a methodical, systematic, and orderly way.

PRIORITIES

- Ensure the crime scene is safe to enter. Check that criminals have left the scene, and carry out safety checks, such as searching for suspicious packages.

- Provide emergency first aid to any injured victims, but avoid washing or removing clothing so as not to destroy possible evidence.

- Protect and secure the crime scene, and establish the crime-scene boundaries, which should include suspects' likely entry and exit points.

- Record evidence and take steps to preserve any perishable evidence.

- Start an evidence log—a list of everybody who studies each piece of evidence. Keep a record of everybody who enters the crime scene.

- Identify witnesses for interviews.

- Document the whole procedure, using notes, sketches, photographs, and possibly videotape.

Sealing the scene

Depending on its size, a crime scene may be cordoned off with crime-scene tape, barricades, vehicles, or police officers.

Taking care

If there are injured people at a crime scene, the first priority is to get them to a hospital. To avoid corrupting any evidence, a CSI will try to determine the suspect's and the victim's entry and exit points and direct paramedics to a different route.

Eyewitness evidence

Ideally, eyewitnesses are interviewed right away, while details of the incident are still fresh. If this is not possible, CSIs will separate the witnesses from each other to prevent them from discussing the incident.

Fingertip search

If the crime scene is small enough, CSIs may carry out a fingertip search for evidence. Kneeling shoulder-to-shoulder and moving forward together, officers search the ground in front of them so that every inch of the crime scene is examined. They wear coveralls, surgical gloves, and masks to prevent contamination from their own clothing or even from their hair or skin particles. Other CSIs photograph, video, and make notes about the crime scene.

In the bag

Before any evidence is removed from the crime scene, it is photographed, its location is recorded, and then it is bagged, sealed, and labeled. Careful record-keeping helps to show that evidence has not been tampered with.

FORENSIC PHOTOGRAPHY

A photograph is said to be worth a thousand words, and this is as true in forensic photography as in any other field. In a court of law, photographs of crime-scene evidence are more reliable than any written or verbal statements could be. It is vital to any criminal investigation that a comprehensive visual record of the crime scene is made quickly, before it can be altered, and meticulously, for absolute accuracy.

Close-ups

Each item of evidence is photographed in close-up to produce detailed records. Items are placed on a white background for maximum visibility, and a written record is kept of the camera settings for each image.

THE SET-UP

- Equipment for producing maximum clarity includes a 35-mm camera. Macro (magnifying) lenses are used for close-ups.

- White paper makes a plain background, to capture more details.

- Scale comparison is used to measure the object and record its true size.

- Tripod keeps the camera steady and at right angles to the object.

- Flash and floodlights are used for capturing greatest detail.

In position

Each piece of evidence is first photographed in the place it was found. Here, a CSI photographs a gun against an evidence marker, so that the gun's exact location is recorded.

Measuring the evidence

In order to record the size of objects, each piece of evidence is photographed against a photographic scale. If a scale is not available, familiar items, such as keys, can give an estimate.

Filming the scene

Video footage of the crime scene might be used to brief other investigators, so fewer people need to enter the scene. The footage may also be produced in a trial to show jurors the crime scene.

Lighting up the evidence

It is especially important that clear photographs are taken of evidence that cannot be removed or might be destroyed. Floodlights have been used to illuminate these tire tracks to show greater detail.

COLLECTING EVIDENCE

CSIs usually have just one opportunity to search a crime scene, so there is no room for error. Quick decisions must be made about exactly what constitutes useful evidence. This becomes more difficult as the field of forensic science widens. Incredibly, even smells can now be packaged and labeled as evidence.

Fast evidence

At a serious crime scene, CSIs mark out key evidence with yellow letter cards. Crime scenes in public places have to be searched quickly so that they can be returned to public access.

PROCEDURE

- Prevent contamination. Searchers wear coveralls and surgical gloves to stop clothing fibers or the searcher's own genetic material from mixing with any evidence found.

- Assess appropriate search type. Depending on the crime and the size and layout of the scene, CSIs may carry out a fingertip or on-foot search, and may use tracker dogs.

- Mark key evidence. Numbered or lettered yellow markers are used to map the location of key pieces of evidence.

Tracker dogs

Dogs are trained to sniff out explosives, illegal drugs, missing people, and corpses. Here, an officer uses a metal probe to assist an underground search. He sticks it into the ground and offers it to the dog to smell the escaping odors.

Swabbing

Tiny spots of suspicious fluids are removed from a crime scene by swabbing. The swabs are taken by an investigator wearing disposable gloves to prevent contamination.

Scent science

A forensic officer uses a device called a Scent Transfer Unit to transmit the human smell from a gun onto a sterile gauze pad. The pad might then be used by dogs to sniff out a suspect, or kept in a scent bank to be used as evidence.

Virtual crime scene

In murder cases the bullet trajectory, or flight path, can be plotted on a 3-D computer model of the crime scene to show investigators where the killer was standing.

YOUR EVIDENCE COLLECTION KIT

To put together your own evidence collection kit, take the items from the jacket of this book and find the other items from around your house. Remember, you should always log your evidence carefully, so find a pen and pad of paper first.

Ink pad ▲
Your vital fingerprinting tool. Use with the paper pad to record suspects' prints.

◀ Sealable bags
Important for preserving small pieces of evidence, such as fibers or hair.

▼ Tweezers
Useful for collecting pieces of trace evidence, such as carpet fibers.

◀ Magnifying glass
This can be used to search for trace evidence and to examine fingerprints and other marks.

◀ Paper pad
For recording fingerprints. Always write down the suspect's name at the top.

Tape measure ▶
So that you can keep a note of the size of pieces of evidence.

ROBBERY
Crime scene analysis

You are called to the scene of a robbery at the Holbrook Gallery. The gallery is housed in the former apartment of 1960s pop-art painter and art collector Stefan Holbrook, and it displays his own paintings and his personal collection of art objects. The gallery's security officer lies unconscious on the floor, and one of the most valuable Holbrook paintings, *Blue Mood*, is missing. Look at the items that CSIs have selected for forensic analysis below, and read up on the tests that will be performed back at the lab. Meanwhile, the police are conducting inquiries. Follow the investigation, then turn to pages 26–7 for the police reports and forensic results. Examine them carefully and see if you can uncover the art thief.

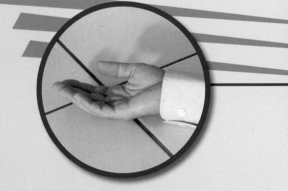

Whose fingerprints?

In the gallery, CSIs are dusting those items that the thief may have touched. Fingerprint examiners will record the prints of the security guard as well as those of everyone else who works in the gallery. See pages 18–21 to find out how investigators recover and match fingerprints.

Suspect liquid?

A hot drink is spilled on the floor beside the unconscious security guard. Could he have been drugged? A sample will be taken to the lab so a toxicologist can run tests. To find out about toxicology, turn to pages 22–3.

CCTV

The closed-circuit television camera has been immobilized. It has been knocked to point up at the ceiling, so it has not recorded the robbery. How did the criminal reach the camera to do this?

Picture frame

The empty picture frame will be carefully examined to find out how the painting was removed. If tool marks or cuts are found, these could be used as evidence. Turn to pages 34–5 to read about tool marks.

Traces of glass

Broken glass from the picture frame litters the sofa and floor. If glass fragments are found on a suspect's clothes or shoes, they could be matched with these crime-scene shards to prove they were at the scene. Read about trace evidence on pages 24–5.

FACT FILE

In 1911, Leonardo da Vinci's *Mona Lisa* was stolen from the Louvre in Paris. One of the gallery's employees had simply walked out with the masterpiece under his coat. Two years later, the painting was recovered. The thief claimed he wanted to return it to Italy.

RECOVERING FINGERPRINTS

Every person on the planet has different patterns on their fingertips—even identical twins. These patterns are evidence of our unique identities, and every time we touch a surface we leave some of this evidence behind, in the form of fingerprints. When criminals leave their fingerprints at a crime scene, the prints are often invisible, or latent. Investigators use a range of techniques to recover them.

Dusting for fingerprints

Fingerprints left on shiny surfaces, such as glass, are the easiest to recover. These surfaces are nonporous, which means they do not absorb moisture. The sweat or grease that our fingers leave behind stays on the surface, and can usually be revealed fairly easily using powders.

Aluminum powder

The investigator dusts the suspect area with aluminum powder using a brush. The powder sticks to moisture left by sweat from the skin's ridges, making the prints visible.

Protecting evidence

Investigators always wear latex gloves to prevent contamination from their own fingerprints.

Lifting fingerprints

The investigator carefully lifts the print with adhesive tape. The print is then mounted onto a transparent sheet so that it can be preserved as evidence.

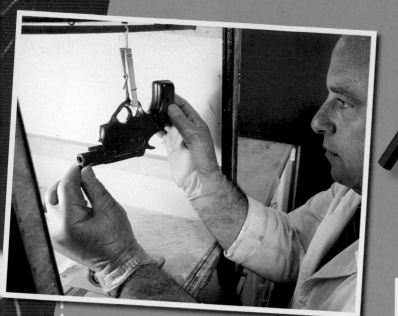

RObBERY CASE ANALYSIS

At the Holbrook Gallery, CSIs are busy lifting fingerprints. All the surfaces are nonporous, and aluminum powder is used in most areas. A light-colored powder is applied to reveal moisture on the darker surfaces, such as the standing lamp.

Superglue fuming

Small items can easily be removed from the crime scene and taken to the laboratory, where different treatments can be used to reveal latent fingerprints. One of these is called superglue fuming. The suspect object is placed in an airtight container, and fans inside it circulate superglue fumes. The glue vapor sticks to the sweat left by fingers, making it visible.

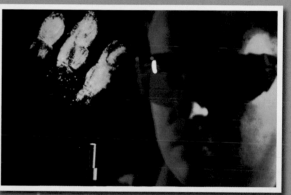

Special illumination

After superglue fuming, chemicals are applied to make the fingerprints glow when certain lights, such as ultraviolet (UV), are shone on them. This improves contrast and enhances the print.

REVEALING FINGERPRINTS

1

2

3

Investigators use aluminum powder to dust for prints on nonporous surfaces, but you can use cocoa powder to do a similar activity at home.

You will need: cocoa powder • mug or drinking glass • small, clean paintbrush • transparent tape • light-colored paper or posterboard

1. First, make a fingerprint on a shiny surface, such as a mug or glass. You will get a clearer fingerprint when more body oils are present, so rub your finger along your nose or through your hair first.

2. Lightly sprinkle the cocoa powder over the fingerprint. Then gently blow or brush the loose powders away, using a soft, clean paintbrush.

3. Lift the print from the mug by placing the sticky side of a piece of tape on the dusted print and then carefully lifting up the tape. Stick the piece of tape onto a sheet of white paper.

N.B. To lift prints from dark surfaces, use talcum powder and stick the print onto dark paper.

Laser beam

Laser light is sometimes used for revealing prints previously treated with a fluorescent powder. Laser light is particularly useful for revealing old fingerprints.

MATCHING PRINTS

Fingerprints have been used to identify suspects for more than a hundred years. But matching prints was a skilled and time-consuming task, which became longer and more difficult still as collections of fingerprints grew. In 1975, the first automated fingerprint identification system (AFIS) revolutionized fingerprint matching. Today, AFIS can search and compare a million records every second.

Fingerprint types

Fingerprints are classified by their basic pattern, of which there are four: whorls, loops, arches, and combinations. Each type is then broken down into further groups according to tiny details, such as the number and direction of ridges.

Loops
Loops are the most common pattern, making up about 60–70% of all fingerprints.

Combination or composite
Characteristics of the other fingerprint types exist together in these rare prints.

Whorls
Around 25% of fingerprint patterns are whorls.

Arches
Only about 5% of fingerprint patterns are arches.

ROBBERY CASE ANALYSIS

All the prints taken at the Holbrook Gallery have now been scanned and added to the AFIS database. AFIS will alert the operator if it locates a match with a known criminal. Prints of all the gallery employees are being scanned, too.

Ink and roll

The traditional, universal method of taking fingerprints is called "ink and roll." The suspect's fingertips are rolled in black ink from one side of the nail to the other. The ink-covered fingertips are then rolled on a white chart to produce prints.

RECORD FINGERPRINTS

You can perform an ink and roll using the items found on the jacket of this book.

You will need: ink pad • fingerprint record pad • magnifying glass

1. Press the fingertip into the ink, rolling from one side to the other so that it is evenly coated.

2. Press and roll the fingertip in the same way onto a sheet from your fingerprint record pad. Make prints of the index fingers of everyone in your family in this way, so you end up with prints on several sheets. Don't forget to write the person's name at the top of each sheet.

3. Examine the prints carefully using your magnifying glass. How many of the four types can you identify? If you have two fingerprints of the same type, can you see differences between them? Note down your results next to each fingerprint.

Fingerprint scanning

Today, fingerprint scanners are taking over from the ink-and-roll method. Fingertips are scanned electronically and added to a computer database. Prints retrieved from a crime scene can be scanned, too. The process is fast, clean, and efficient.

Unique features

Fingerprint examiners look at two main features: bifurcations (a)—the places where the ridges divide into two—and the ridge endings (b). The directions of the ridges in the bifurcations and where ridges begin and end are noted. A fingerprint expert will select a number of these tiny details and then give his or her expert opinion on whether or not there is a match.

Computer matching

Automated fingerprint identification systems (AFIS) plot the features of a crime-scene fingerprint and compare them with the characteristics of all the fingerprints in their database. These systems cannot come up with one perfect match, but present a list of the closest ones. Fingerprint experts then study the results to confirm a match.

TOXICOLOGY

The human body retains traces of everything that is ingested, sometimes for months afterward. Toxicologists are trained to find and analyze these traces, in order to identify athletes using performance-enhancing drugs, illegal drug users, or, more rarely, victims of poisoning. A snip of hair, a drop of blood, a deep breath—all can reveal chemical abuse.

ROBBERY CASE ANALYSIS

A sample of the spilled tea from the Holbrook Gallery is now awaiting analysis at the toxicology lab. An immunoassay test will be carried out and, if positive, further tests will establish the nature of the drug or poison present.

Testing hair

Here, a technician prepares a sample of hair for drug testing in a toxicology lab. Traces of chemicals from drugs and poisons are stored in the hair shaft, and they stay in a fixed position as the hair grows. So, long hair cut from the scalp can contain a timeline of drug history.

Lock of hair
The hair is taped to a record sheet on which the suspected drug user's details are recorded.

Vials
Each hair sample is placed into a vial. A solvent is then added to draw out any drug extracts.

Hair sample
The hair is cut into $1/3$-inch (1-cm) pieces to make a calendar of drug use.

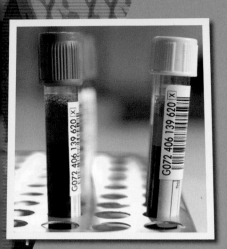

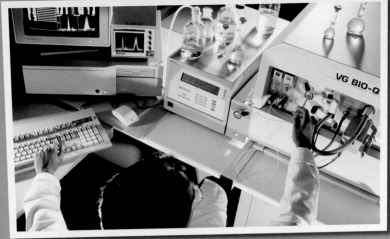

Drug test

The simplest, most common drug test is usually carried out on blood or urine with an immunoassay kit. If drugs or poisons are present, the sample changes color when mixed with the kit's chemicals.

Measuring quantities

Two machines linked together—a gas chromatograph and a mass spectrometer (GC/MS)—measure exact quantities of drugs or poisons present. Liquid samples are inserted and the results appear as a series of colored peaks on a screen.

Blow here

The most common toxicological test measures a legal drug, alcohol, and is carried out at the side of the road. The breathalyzer measures the amount of alcohol in drivers' breath.

TEST CHEMICAL CHARACTERISTICS

⚠ Ask an adult to boil the red cabbage

To identify an unknown substance, forensic scientists perform many tests. One is to test for chemical characteristics—whether a substance is acid or alkaline. Here, cabbage water is used as a chemical indicator: acid will turn it red, alkalines turn it purple.

You will need: a saucepan • a colander • a pitcher • some clean water • 2 red cabbage leaves • 3 tablespoons (45 ml) lemon juice • 3 tablespoons (45 ml) vinegar • 1 tablespoon (15 ml) baking soda

1

1. Fill a saucepan with 1½ quarts (1.5 liters) of water. Tear the cabbage leaves into small pieces and add them to the pan. Ask an adult to boil the water for 5 minutes, then allow to cool for half an hour and strain into a pitcher.

2

2. Take three glass tumblers and label them from 1 to 3. Divide the cabbage water equally between the three tumblers.

3

3. Add the lemon juice to jar 1, the vinegar to jar 2, and the baking soda to jar 3. Note down the color that each substance turns the cabbage water. Now you can tell which substance is acid and which is alkaline.

Chemical attack

Poison attacks carried out by terrorists in order to kill and cause panic are a real threat. In 1995, a nerve gas attack on Tokyo's subway killed 12 and injured thousands.

TRACE EVIDENCE

Locard's exchange principle—"every contact leaves a trace"—is the idea behind trace evidence. At a crime scene, there will be traces of the criminal, and the fleeing criminal will unwittingly carry away traces of evidence from the scene. Tiny particles, such as hairs, clothing fibers, flecks of paint, or soil, can link a suspect to a crime scene and may even enable police to nail a criminal.

Tracking traces

A criminal always leaves some trace evidence at a crime scene. Investigators have to be especially vigilant to find the tiny specks and fragments that could be vital evidence.

Tell-tale hair

A strand of hair can be used to link a suspect to the scene, if the color can be matched. If the hair root is present, DNA could be extracted. Many criminals wear hats to keep from leaving hairs at the scene.

Shedding evidence

Our clothing sheds tiny fibers all the time. To find a match between a crime scene and a suspect sample, experts examine minute details such as the diameter and shape of each fiber, the shape of the weave and the number of fibers it contains, and the type of dye used.

Shoe traces

Footprints left at a crime scene can add to evidence against a suspect. A shoe sole containing traces of carpet fiber or flecks of paint that match those at the crime scene is much more incriminating.

Paint layers

Vehicle paintwork is often applied in three layers, and police keep databases of manufacturers' compositions and color ranges. A link can be made if a crime-scene and suspect sample have identical layers.

Collecting traces

Wearing gloves to prevent contamination, CSIs use a suction device, much like a tiny household vacuum cleaner, to collect hair and fiber trace evidence. The material is sucked onto a filter paper, which is then placed in a sealed, labeled plastic bag ready for analysis in the lab. If hairs and fibers are concentrated in a small area, CSIs may lift them with tape.

Electron microscope

Sometimes, objects are removed to the lab for analysis. Experts examine traces under an electron microscope to identify them and study their surface detail. Here, a researcher examines traces of powder on clothing. Electron microscopes can reveal details 10,000 times smaller than a hair's breadth.

WHERE HAS A SUSPECT BEEN?

1

2

This activity shows how you might be able to find out where a suspect has been by analyzing seeds on their shoes and clothes.

<u>You will need:</u> an old pair of socks • tweezers • white paper • magnifying glass

1. Put an old pair of socks over your shoes and walk around your yard, or ask an adult to go with you to the local park. Back at home, pick off any seeds stuck to your socks with tweezers and put them onto a piece of white paper.

2. Examine the seeds with your magnifying glass and sort them into types. How many different types are there? Can you identify which plants they came from? Ask an adult to help you, or plant the seeds in soil-filled pots to see what plants sprout.

ROBBERY CASE ANALYSIS

In the lab, forensic experts are examining the clothing worn by the Holbrook Gallery's employees on the day of the robbery. Any fragments of glass in the seams of a jacket or the soles of a shoe could be incriminating evidence.

ROBBERY

Case Overview

Suspect Profile

Name: Karen Shooter

Age: 52

- Art dealer. Had been pursuing the painting for months on behalf of a wealthy client.

- Was at the gallery that afternoon, meeting with the director to make another offer on the painting, Blue Mood.

- Police records show that she was recently under suspicion of dealing in stolen artworks, but there was not enough evidence to prosecute.

Name: Karen Shooter

Finger: Index finger

* Selling stolen artworks is not easy, especially if they are very famous, but Shooter would have the contacts to do it like this ike

Suspect Profile

Name: Ed Kolowski

Age: 45

- Director of the Holbrook Gallery.

- Spent the afternoon with Karen Shooter, from 3:30 pm until she left at 4:40 pm. Remained in his office until 5:10 pm when he entered the main gallery and discovered the crime scene.

- On the verge of bankruptcy due to his extravagant lifestyle.

Name: Ed Kolowski

Finger: Index finger

Would Kolowski really steal from his own gallery, even if he desperately needed the money?

Art thieves strike again!

BY FRAN BAINES

Blue Mood, a valuable work by pop-art painter Stefan Holbrook, has disappeared from the Holbrook Gallery in the center of town.

The painting was removed from the wall of the gallery's second exhibition room late in the afternoon. Police are perplexed as to how the thief was able to leave unseen.

This is the third in a series of high-profile art robberies from various galleries in the city. Police believe they were inside jobs, but so far have not been able to prove it.

Fingerprint Report

Fingerprint lifted from the lamp in the Holbrook Gallery

Print of index finger found at the scene

Fingerprints belonging to all four suspects were found in the gallery, but only one set was found on the lamp used to disable the CCTV camera.

Compare the print lifted from the scene, left, to those of the four suspects to find out who moved the camera.

POLICE NOTES

The gallery has only one point of entry, via the reception. All the windows were locked and there was no sign of tampering.

<u>4:15</u> Last group of visitors leaves the building. The painting is still on the wall.

<u>4:30</u> Jimmy O'Brien takes his tea into the gallery.

<u>4:40</u> Karen Shooter leaves the building.

<u>5:10</u> The crime scene is discovered by Ed Kolowski.

Suspect Profile

Name: Jimmy O'Brien

Age: 37

- Security guard at the gallery, found unconscious at the crime scene.

- He says at 4:20 pm he went to the kitchen to make a cup of tea, but left the cup unattended for a few moments as he went to the bathroom. Took the tea back to the main gallery but started to feel faint and then collapsed. He can recall nothing more.

- Has only worked at the gallery for a few months and has kept himself to himself.

Name: Jimmy O'Brien
Finger: Index finger

How did the thief get the painting out of the building?

Trace Evidence

Traces of paint and glass analyzed

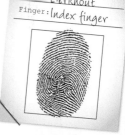

Traces of white paint were found on the lamp in the gallery. Tests show the paint came from the security camera on the ceiling, suggesting the lamp was used to knock the camera away.

No tool marks were found on the picture frame. The painting was simply unclipped from its frame.

All the suspects' shoes and clothing were examined for trace evidence. Microscopic fragments of glass were found embedded in the shoes of two of the suspects—Jimmy O'Brien and Ed Kolowski.

HOLBROOK GALLERY FLOOR PLAN

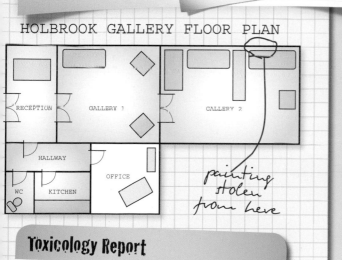

RECEPTION GALLERY 1 GALLERY 2

HALLWAY

OFFICE

WC KITCHEN

painting stolen from here

Suspect Profile

Name: Anna Berkhout

Age: 23

- Art Student, works part-time as a receptionist at the gallery.

- Says she was at the reception all afternoon. The last group of visitors left at 4:15 pm, and no one else left the building after Karen Shooter at 4:40 pm.

- Loves Holbrook's work and is critical of the director.

Name: Anna Berkhout
Finger: Index finger

Once chained herself to a famous painting after it was set to be sold to a bidder in another country

Toxicology Report

Analysis of tea spills near body of Jimmy O'Brien

The spilled tea found next to Jimmy O'Brien's body was analyzed and found to contain traces of a sedative drug, easily available over the counter in most pharmacies.

The level found was sufficient to induce a deep sleep but was not enough to cause serious harm.

Who could have spiked the tea? How did they know he would make a cup?

Who has traces that link them to the scene?

SCENE ARSON CRIME SCE

YouR wareHouse is going up
in flames if you don't

ARSON

Crime scene analysis

A late night phone call informs you of a suspicious fire at the Glad Rags Clothing Company's warehouse. Luckily, a passerby saw the flames and called the fire department before too much damage was caused. CSIs arrived on the scene early the next morning and have identified some suspicious items for analysis by forensics. It looks as though the fire was started deliberately. Take a look at the items, below, and see if you agree. You'll need to read up on the relevant forensic tests to see what these clues might reveal. As forensic tests are carried out, the police will be interviewing all those connected with the warehouse, as well as the passerby. The results appear on pages 38–9. Check them out and see if you can identify the arsonist.

Forced entry

The lock on the door has been broken with a crowbar or other large tool. The damage to the door frame might tell investigators what kind of tool was used. Find out how on pages 34–5.

Muddy shoeprints

A clearly visible shoeprint could be an important piece of evidence if it can be matched to a suspect's shoe. See pages 34–5 for more about shoeprints.

Fire starter

A cigar has been lit and discarded on the floor, close to the seat, or origin, of the fire. Could it have been used to start the blaze? Could it prove a link with any of the suspects? Turn to pages 32–3 to find out about investigating fires.

Computer hard drive

The computer is to be removed immediately, and its hard drive examined by forensic experts. It could hold clues to a possible motive. See pages 36–7 to find out about computer forensics.

Poison pen letter

A letter threatening arson lies on the desk, undamaged by the fire. The handwriting will be analyzed and compared with that of any suspects. Turn to pages 36–7 to read about document forensics.

Accelerant

Investigators have identified the seat, or origin, of the fire. They will test the air around the seat for traces of gasoline or other accelerants. Samples of partly burned clothing and furniture will be taken to the lab for analysis. Go to pages 32–3 to read about the techniques used.

FACT FILE

In 2004, a devastating fire tore through a London warehouse containing priceless works of modern art. The blaze was so destructive that experts claimed it was impossible to tell whether the fire was accidental or incendiary (deliberate).

FIRES AND BOMB BLASTS

When a fire rips through a building or a bomb blast tears it apart, the crime scene will be severely damaged. Efforts to extinguish the flames may make matters worse, leaving just a charred wreck for the forensic investigators. But even the most fire-damaged building is likely to contain clues. After an explosion, bomb fragments and traces of explosives can help investigators trace the culprits.

Fighting the flames

Firefighters' first priority is, of course, to save lives, but their second is incident stabilization—to preserve the crime scene as much as possible.

Canine detector

Over the last decades, arson investigators have started using trained sniffer dogs to detect accelerants.

Tools of the trade

Fire investigators' equipment helps them negotiate unsafe buildings and remove evidence.

Flashlight

In a fire-damaged building, usually unsafe and without lighting, the simple flashlight is an essential tool.

Gas analysis kit

This device is used to detect the presence of accelerant at the scene. Crystals inside the tube change color when traces of accelerant are present in the air drawn through it.

Ax and chainsaw

An ax is used to remove parts of structures inside fire-damaged buildings for examination elsewhere. Chainsaws may be used to remove flooring soaked in accelerant, for analysis back in the lab.

Sifting through charred remains

To investigate a fire, patterns of soot are followed to their origin, or "seat." Accidental fires usually start in one place, so more than one seat is suspicious. Once the seat is located, investigators look for traces of accelerant.

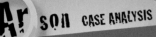 **Arson** CASE ANALYSIS

At the crime scene, CSIs deduced that the fire was probably incendiary (deliberate). In the area where the fire started, they found a partly burned cigar, a likely incendiary device. They also suspect that an accelerant has been used.

Forensic analysis

Remains suspected of containing accelerants are taken to the lab in sealed glass jars. There, scientists detect any accelerants using a technique called mass spectrometry, which identifies chemicals by the mass of their molecules.

MAKE A FIRE EXTINGUISHER

Fire needs three things in order to burn—heat, fuel, and oxygen. Carbon dioxide is more dense than oxygen, meaning things can't burn in it. This makes it an ideal material for a fire extinguisher.

<u>You will need:</u> small candle • shallow bowl • match • bottle • bicarbonate of soda • vinegar

1. Place the candle into the shallow bowl and carefully light the wick. Mix the ingredients for your fire extinguisher by pouring the bicarbonate of soda into a bottle, followed by some vinegar.

2. The mixture will fizz and give off carbon dioxide, an invisible gas. Make sure you cover the bottle with your thumb to hold in the carbon dioxide gas.

3. To extinguish the flame, carefully bring the open end of the bottle over the burning candle and remove your thumb. The dense carbon dioxide gas sweeps away the oxygen, putting out the fire.

Ask an adult to supervise as you light the candle

Anatomy of a bomb

Members of the Irish Republican Army made this bomb with batteries, lighter fuel, and a circuit board. Fragments of bomb components, collected after an explosion, can sometimes be traced to their source.

TRACKS AND MARKS

Most criminals take precautions to avoid detection. They might wear gloves so they don't leave fingerprints, masks to cover their faces, and hats to avoid shedding hairs. But the shoes criminals wear, the tools they use, and their getaway vehicles can all leave distinctive marks at the crime scene. These marks are clues that forensic investigators are sometimes able to turn into hard evidence.

Tire tracks

In a rural area, a getaway car fleeing from the crime scene is likely to leave tire tracks. By measuring the distance between the two lines of tracks and the width of each tread mark, investigators can tell what type of vehicle the tracks came from.

Tire cast

A cast of tire tracks might be made after they have been photographed. If the tires are worn, they will produce unique marks, which will show up clearly on the cast.

Tool marks

Damage to a window frame by a burglar's screwdriver may not seem like important evidence. But differences in the manufacturing process and wear from use mean that no two tools are alike, so they all leave different impressions. Casts can be made of tool marks (usually in the lab), making comparisons with suspect tools easier.

Wear and tear

The same scuffs and marks have been identified on this crime-scene print (right), and a suspect's shoe sole (left). To prove a link, investigators must find the same marks of wear and tear on both.

Arson CASE ANALYSIS

The tool marks on the door frame are analyzed for unique marks, and the muddy shoeprint is photographed and scanned into the shoe database. No match with other crime-scene prints is found, but the print may still match one of the suspects' shoes.

Shoe database

Records of crime-scene shoeprints and of manufacturers' sole styles are stored on databases, allowing investigators to identify shoe styles and to match prints found at crime scenes to those of known criminals.

MAKE A CAST OF YOUR SHOEPRINT

Investigators make casts of shoeprints left at a crime scene in order to study the unique marks that might lead to a suspect. This activity shows you how to make a cast of your own shoeprint, using plaster of Paris.

You will need: a well-worn sneaker • plaster of Paris • water • an old shoe box with the bottom cut out • soft soil • brush • magnifying glass

1. First make a footprint in the soil, wearing your old sneaker. Surround it with the bottomless shoe box.

2. Mix the plaster of Paris with water according to the instructions and pour over the shoeprint. Leave the plaster to dry for about one hour.

3. Take the cast out and bring it indoors. Leave it to harden overnight on a piece of newspaper. Brush the loose soil off and look at your cast using your magnifying glass. Can you identify any unique marks? Make casts of friends' prints and compare them.

Banking fraud

Here, fraud squad officers study a bank's computer records. Siphoning off tiny amounts of money from thousands of bank accounts, known as the "one-half-cent crime," has become a popular banking fraud.

Accessing the memory bank

A computer's hard drive is its memory. All the data composed on the computer, including material that has been deleted, is stored there, at least temporarily. When a computer is seized, investigators make a copy of the hard drive in order to avoid corrupting the original.

Forensic Analysis

COMPUTER AND DOCUMENT FORENSICS

From bank fraud to hacking, the massive increase in computer use means that many crimes are now committed in cyberspace. Criminals planning a conventional crime are likely to use computers, too. Computer forensics is a new science combatting computer-related crime. Document examiners have also been extending their expertise—literary forensics is another field that is opening up in the fight against crime.

MAKE A CHROMATOGRAPHY TEST

Chromatography is a technique used by scientists to separate the components of a mixture. It can help investigators to identify different inks, because even inks of the same color are made up of different quantities of colored pigments.

You will need: coffee filter paper cut into strips 1 inch (2–3 cm) wide • three water-soluble felt-tipped pens • three glasses or jars containing about $^1/_3$ inch (1 cm) of tap water • paperclips • pencil • a piece of paper towel

1. Color a circle ½ inch (1–2 cm) from the end of one of the coffee filter strips. For each pen, take a new coffee filter strip and color another circle.

2. Attach each strip to a glass so that the bottom of the strip touches the water. The water should not quite reach the circle you've drawn. Watch as the water creeps up the paper strip and reaches the top.

3. Take the strips out of the water and place them on a piece of paper towel. You will see that the ink colors have separated into different patterns, called chromatography patterns.

Literary analysis

Handwriting experts assess whether two documents, such as the signatures shown left, were written by the same person. They study spacing, letter heights, and slope. When anonymous letters are received by police, a literary forensics expert may examine the type of language used to establish the author's identity.

REAL

Thomas A. Edison

Thomas Edison

FAKE

Arson CASE ANALYSIS

The poison pen letter is a valuable piece of evidence. A handwriting expert is examining the shape of the letters to find a match with suspects' writing. Investigators copied the computer hard drive and are studying its contents.

Revealing an impression

Writing on a pad of paper impresses a copy onto the following sheet. Some people press the pen hard, making a visible copy, but when the impression is very light an electrostatic detection apparatus (ESDA) can reveal it. Toner is dusted onto the suspect sheet (a), and a static charge is applied that sucks the toner into the indentations (b), showing the indented writing.

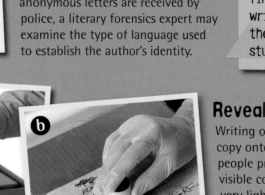

ARSON

Case Overview

Computer Forensics Report

Financial data found on the hard drive

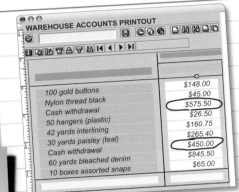

WAREHOUSE ACCOUNTS PRINTOUT	
	$148.00
100 gold buttons	$45.00
Nylon thread black	$575.50
Cash withdrawal	$26.50
50 hangers (plastic)	$160.75
42 yards interlining	$265.40
30 yards paisley (teal)	$450.00
Cash withdrawal	$845.50
60 yards bleached denim	$65.00
10 boxes assorted snaps	

An examination of the computer hard drive shows that the company is in severe financial difficulty. However, it also looks as though someone has been siphoning off money from the company accounts over a long period of time. The spreadsheet on the left shows some of the large cash withdrawals.

Suspect Profile

Name: Michael Beasley

Age: 37

- The passerby who was taking a late night walk when he spotted the blaze and alerted the fire department. The warehouse is at an industrial park, far from the town center and Beasley's home.

- He's a petty criminal, known to the police for theft and vandalism charges.

* What was he doing in the area so late at night? Arsonists sometimes stay at the scene of their crimes, alerting the fire department in order to become the "hero"...

Suspect Profile

Name: Karl Caudwell

Age: 49

- Manager of the warehouse, has worked there for years.

- Responsible for the day-to-day running of the business and all the bookkeeping.

- Says he was at home with his wife, Louise, at the time of the fire, but they were both in bed asleep.

NB: Not a reliable alibi.

Fire Investigator's Report

Cigar found at the crime scene

The samples of burned material showed traces of an accelerant, probably gasoline. Empty gas cans were found outside the building, but they had no fingerprints on them.

The fire was probably ignited with the cigar found at the scene. Investigators deduced that the cigar was lit and flicked onto the gas-soaked boxes of stock.

`Cigar found at scene`

WITNESS STATEMENT

Joyce Evans—Cleaner

She says there was a fight the night before the fire. Richard Gibbs showed up at the warehouse and there was a heated exchange between him and Katherine Holden. He wanted her to sell the company to him at a rock-bottom price. She said she knew she'd have to sell, but it would never be to him. Karl Caudwell was also present.

Suspect Profile

Name: Katherine Holden
AGE: 32

- Owner of Glad Rags.
- Admits that the company was in serious trouble and she was in danger of losing her house.
- Stands to cash in on big insurance claim.
- Mentions her fight with Richard Gibbs the night before, says he was aggressive.
- Confirms she received a malicious letter threatening arson on the day of the fire. She assumed it was from Richard Gibbs.
- Says she had been at the warehouse earlier in the evening but claims to have been at home in bed at the time of the arson.

Marks and Tracks

Footprints and toolmarks left behind by the arsonist

An examination of the marks around the door frame shows that it was forced open with a crowbar. A crowbar that could have made these marks was found outside Richard Gibbs's garage.

The shoeprints found at the scene were smudged but the clearest was photographed and is shown in this picture.

Did one of the suspects leave this print?

YouR wareHouse is going up in FLames if you don't Sell Up.

Ignore this at your peril!!!

The poison pen letter found at crime scene

Document Forensics

Poison pen letter

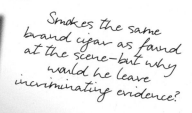

Yours,

L

No match was found between the handwriting on the poison pen letter and samples taken from each of the four suspects.

However, use of an ESDA machine revealed an impression of indented writing on the paper the letter was written on (see left). No match was found with this handwriting either, and none of the suspects' names begin with L.

Suspect Profile

Name: Richard Gibbs
AGE: 41

- Owner of rival clothing company, Allstar Apparel.
- Common knowledge that he wants to put his rival out of business.
- Was at a charity auction on the night of the fire, on the other side of town. Last seen half an hour before the fire department was called to put out the blaze.

Smokes the same brand cigar as found at the scene—but why would he leave incriminating evidence?

FORGERY

Crime scene analysis

Police making a regular patrol in the area spot unusual activity at the Night Fly Printers' workshop on a Sunday afternoon. The door is wide open, and the policeman enters. He can hardly believe his eyes: piles of forged bills are stacked up around the room. The press, which usually prints catalogs and leaflets, is churning out counterfeit cash. Turning to the window, the policeman glimpses a shadowy figure outside. He calls you to the crime scene. Look below to see what the team of CSIs has identified for forensic analysis. Follow the investigation, then when you're ready, go to pages 50–1 for the full reports, and use your detective skills to finger the forger.

Eyewitness

The person outside was out walking his dog when, as the police car approached, he saw someone run out of Night Fly's back door. Police will see if he can help them with their inquiries. Read about eyewitness evidence on pages 46–7.

Computer hard drive

A laptop screen displays a forged bill. Forensic experts will copy and examine the hard disk to find out what role it played in the crime. See pages 36–7 for more on computer forensics.

Serial numbers

Real bills are numbered sequentially, but forgeries carry the same serial numbers. This is one of a number of security features that are usually missing from forged bills. To find out more about fake money and how to spot it, take a look at pages 44–5.

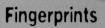

Fingerprints

The press is covered with prints. These will be matched against the prints of Night Fly's employees. To read about how investigators recover and match fingerprints, turn to pages 18–21.

Supplies

The forger needed paper and inks to commit the crime. If investigators can find out where these came from, it could take them one step closer to catching the criminal.

Bloodstain

A suspicious stain covers some of the bills. It looks as if the forger has cut him or herself on the machinery. But this is just a hunch, and scientific evidence is needed to back it up, so the money will be taken to a serology lab for forensic testing. Find out about serology tests on pages 48–9.

FACT FILE

US-born master con-artist Frank Abagnale forged checks to the tune of $2.5 million in the 1960s. Abagnale started his forgery career aged only 16 and by age 21 he was wanted in 26 countries. He now advises banks on how to avoid fraudsters.

FAKES AND FORGERIES

Publishing software—the same that produced this book—and computer printers and scanners have made currency forgery relatively simple. Counterfeit goods are produced in huge quantities and sold all over the world. Famous paintings change hands for tens of millions of dollars, making forging them hugely profitable. Forensic investigators and detectives work together to find the forgeries and foil the fakes.

Making money

These euro notes were all identified as fakes by experts. Banks continue to introduce more sophisticated security features on money to fight currency forgery. Although these could be copied, it would be so expensive to do so that it would make the forgery unprofitable.

Intaglio

An expensive printing technique, intaglio uses engraved plates to produce a raised image. Other, cheaper printing techniques do not produce the same results and can easily be spotted.

Holograms

Three-dimensional images visible on a flat surface—holograms—have been used as a security feature on currency since 1989. They are produced by a unique photographic process and are very difficult to replicate.

Security thread

It is very difficult to fake the metal thread that is woven through, or printed onto, the paper. Some paper currency, such as the US dollar bill, also has text identifying the bill's denomination printed along the thread for additional security.

Art forgery

British artist Tom Keating, shown here in his studio, claimed to have produced more than 2,000 paintings in the style of various famous artists. Ironically, after his death, his forged works became valuable collectibles in their own right.

Fo rgery CASE ANALYSIS

Counterfeit experts are examining the fake bills discovered at Night Fly now. They are looking at them to see how good the copies are, and by exactly what methods they were produced. This will help them to spot similar jobs in the future.

Scanning for fakes

Passport scanners shine an ultraviolet light to detect hidden security features that would be missing on a fake. They can enhance the portrait to check for tampering and can connect to a wanted people database.

CAN YOU SPOT THE FORGERY?

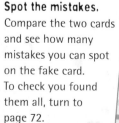

STUDENT IDENTIFICATION CARD

STUDENT

FIRST NAME: Juan
LSAT NAME: Castalino

Juan Castalino

DATE ISSUED:
04/31/2007

SIC

9664 664 5647 483

It is difficult to make perfect forgeries and trained investigators will easily spot mistakes.

Look closely at the cards. Can you tell which one is the authentic identity document and which one is the fake? Take a look at the security features.

Spot the mistakes. Compare the two cards and see how many mistakes you can spot on the fake card. To check you found them all, turn to page 72.

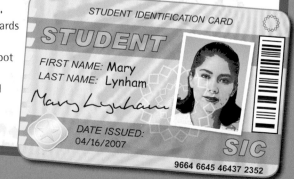

STUDENT IDENTIFICATION CARD

STUDENT

FIRST NAME: Mary
LAST NAME: Lynham

Mary Lynham

DATE ISSUED:
04/16/2007

SIC

9664 6645 46437 2352

Counterfeit watches

A US customs agent drives a steam roller over 17,000 fake designer watches. Many people will buy a fake Rolex watch for a fraction of the real price. But the market in counterfeit goods robs designers of copyright fees and helps fund organized crime.

IDENTIFYING A CRIMINAL

Criminals are rarely convicted by forensic evidence alone. In court, identification by an eyewitness or CCTV footage carries more weight than footprints in mud or stray hairs left at a crime scene. Without eyewitnesses, detectives identify their suspects by eliminating the innocent. Once a suspect is in the interview room, the job of finding out whether they have something to hide begins.

Forgery CASE ANALYSIS

Sam Barnes, who saw someone running from the scene as he passed the Night Fly warehouse, is now with a detective at the local police station. Using special computer software, he is creating a likeness of the face he saw.

Profiling
The way that crimes are committed can tell investigators whether the culprits are career criminals or wayward teenagers. Studying patterns in the methods of repeat offenders can help investigators to identify the criminal.

Caught on camera
Closed-circuit television (CCTV) can prove that a criminal was at a crime scene. Some systems use facial recognition software to match the faces of people filmed against photographs of criminals in its database.

IDENTIFYING SUSPECTS BY ELIMINATION

Entire Population

1. Before any elimination, everyone is a suspect.

All men

2. All women may be eliminated, reducing the pool by half.

Men aged 15-35

3. Those under 15 and over 35 years old may be eliminated.

Men aged 15-35, over 6 ft tall

4. All those under 6 ft (1.8 m) tall may be eliminated

Defining the search

Narrowing down a pool of possible suspects to a few individuals is achieved through a process of elimination. Physical characteristics such as gender, height, and age quickly reduce the pool. If any unusual features, such as left-handedness, are known, detectives can narrow the pool much further.

Recreating a face

Modern software allows an eyewitness to recreate the face of a suspect by putting individual features together. The computer holds a massive database of features, so that a likeness can be made. The flaw in the system is the witness's memory—eyewitness identifications are famously unreliable.

Lie detector

When a suspect is interviewed, officers need to find out if he or she is telling the truth. A polygraph, shown left, monitors a speaker's heart rate and blood pressure, which are likely to increase when the person is lying.

ARE YOU A GOOD WITNESS?

Being a good witness is not as easy as it may seem. Follow the instructions below to test how good your powers of observation and description are.

Which suspect?

Choose one of the three pictures on the right. Study it closely for a minute and then cover it up. From memory, describe the physical characterstics of the person to a friend. Your friend should draw a picture of the person you've described. Can your friend tell which one of the pictures you were describing? How similar is his/her picture to the one you picked?

Suspect 1

Suspect 2

Suspect 3

SEROLOGY

The science of serology aims to identify a suspect through bodily fluids. Although sweat, tears, and other bodily fluids may all be examined, blood is more usually found at a crime scene. When analyzing blood, serologists seek to answer three questions: Is it blood? Is the blood human? Whose blood is it? Since the discovery of blood groups, many differences within them have been found, making blood analysis an exacting tool in a criminal investigation.

Testing time

At the lab, serologists carry out a series of tests on blood samples. A presumptive test determines whether a sample is blood. If this is positive, a precipitin test establishes that the blood is human. Then, the ABO test determines blood group.

Is the blood human?

The precipitin test involves introducing an antibody that locks on to human blood in the sample. If the test is negative, antibodies that lock on to the blood of different animals can be introduced to find out what animal the blood came from.

Blood traces

Sometimes, items like this handgun are removed from the crime scene and taken to the lab, where they can be examined for blood traces more methodically. If traces are found, presumptive tests are carried out.

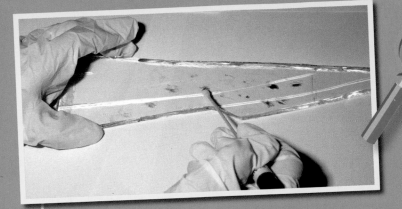

Crime scene test

At the crime scene, CSIs may collect samples of blood for lab analysis (as above) and carry out a presumptive test to find out if a stain is blood. A tab moistened with a test chemical is rubbed onto the stain. If the tip of the tab turns from yellow to green, the stain is blood.

Fo rgery CASE ANALYSIS

The bloodstained notes have been removed from Night Fly and taken to a serology lab. A serologist will carry out three tests—presumptive, precipitin, and ABO. Once the blood group is known, the stain could become an important piece of evidence.

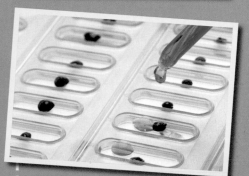

Showing up blood

A chemical called luminol is capable of exposing tiny quantities of blood, so even bloodstains that have been scrubbed can sometimes be revealed. Here, what looks like a clean carpet (far left) is shown to have the impression of a bloody footprint (left).

ABO test

There are four major blood groups: A, B, AB, and O. To find out which group a sample belongs to, scientists carry out this test. A serum is dropped onto the samples, which react in specific ways depending on their group.

REVEAL SECRET MESSAGES

Forensic scientists use chemical reactions to reveal bloodstains that have been washed away. This activity shows you how to make and reveal your own secret messages. It works because the iodine reacts with the paper, but not on the areas masked by the lemon juice.

You will need: a friend • lemon juice • water • iodine tincture • pump spray bottle • white paper • thin clean paintbrush

1. Ask your friend to paint a short message on a piece of white paper, using the paintbrush dipped in the lemon juice. Wait for the paper to dry.

2. Put some water in the spray bottle and mix in a little iodine. Spray the mixture evenly onto the paper, being careful not to use too much.

3. The secret message should be revealed! Tell your friend what you think he or she wrote, then swap roles and draw a secret symbol or write a message yourself.

⚠️ Do not swallow iodine—it may make you sick!

FORGERY

Case Overview

Identification Report

e-fit picture provided by eyewitness

Sam Barnes, the eyewitness on the scene, has given the police a description of the person he saw. He didn't get a very good look, but police have put together an e-fit with his help (see left).

Could this be one of the suspects?

Suspect Profile

Name: Pete Morelli

Age: 34

Blood Group: O

Name: *Pete Morelli*
Finger: *Index finger*

- Owner and manager of Night Fly printers. He owns several other small and mostly unprofitable businesses.

- Drives a brand new sports car and owns a second home abroad.

- Was booked on an early morning flight to his vacation home the day following the crime.

- He claims to have been with his accountant at the time the crime was taking place, and to have no knowledge of the crime at the workshop.

WARNING: Forged bills recovered!

TOM ROBINSON

Several stores and businesses in the area have admitted to receiving forged notes in recent weeks. Police have warned local businesses that these bills are in circulation. The counterfeit bills are good enough to pass a cursory inspection, but police are advising people to check for security features to make sure any note they are handed is genuine.

Suspect Profile

Name: Ray Wallace

Age: 55

Blood Group: B

Name: *Ray Wallace*
Finger: *Index finger*

- The production worker at Night Fly. Has only worked there for three months.

- A very hard worker, but a police search reveals he has a criminal record for fraud, which he did not reveal to his employer.

- Says he was at home by himself at the time of the incident.

*Very nervous during police interview. Is this just because of his criminal record, or has he got something else to hide?

Computer Forensics Report

Examination of the computer hard drive

The criminal has used the company's publishing software to enhance the scan of the bill.

Examination of the hard drive has turned up several deleted files—earlier versions of the bills made by the forger. They were all created by someone going by the username "Monday."

Is this username a clue to the culprit?

Suspect Profile

Name: Erin Lee
Age: 32
Blood Group: A

- Night Fly's graphic designer.

- Has worked at the company part-time for 18 months. Keeps to herself.

- Admits that she is a gambler and has big debts. Needs money quickly.

- Claims to have been at the races at the time.

Has all the expertise necessary to put together the forgery

Name: *Erin Lee*
Finger: *Index finger*

Fingerprint Report

Prints lifted from scene of crime

Three distinct sets of fingerprints were recovered from around the scene. The clearest were found on the printing press (see right).

It's likely that one of the prints belongs to the culprit. Check the suspects' prints and see if you can find whose matches.

Report on Forged Bill

Note found at scene

Bills recovered from the scene

- The counterfeit bills found at the crime scene match the ones already found in circulation in the local area.
- The copies have been made by scanning real currency, improving the image using software, then running them out on the press in huge numbers.
- The paper and inks used in the process were ordered through the company account with the company's usual supplier.

The culprit must have had access to the firm's accounts

Suspect Profile

Name: Monica Day
Age: 25
Bloodgroup: A

- The PA at Night Fly.

- Started a graphic design course but dropped out. Now sometimes helps Erin with the design work.

- Has an expensive lifestyle given her poorly paid job.

Name: *Monica Day*
Finger: *Index finger*

Serology Report

Bloodstains from scene of crime

The stain on the forged bills at the scene was swabbed and taken for analysis at the lab.

The stains were found to be human blood, and further tests revealed them to belong to blood group A.

Looks like the forger cut him/herself. Could clumsiness suggest inexperience with the equipment?

Blood found at scene

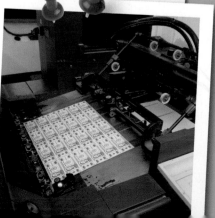

MURDER
Crime scene analysis

Landscaping work on the grounds of Beech House has stopped abruptly after a grisly discovery: a human skeleton has been found buried beneath an old rock garden. You arrive at the country house with the team of CSIs, ready to investigate. No one knows how long the skeleton has lain there, but the house has been in the same family for more than a hundred years, so family history may hold a clue. Soon you discover that 25-year-old Jack Macadie disappeared in 1918 and was never seen again. Could the skeleton be his? Look at the clues below, then study the full investigation on pages 62–3. Find out who the victim is, then track down the murderer.

Skull

A hole in the skull looks like a bullet wound, and this is confirmed when a bullet is found inside the skull. The bullet will be examined in the lab by a firearms expert. For more on firearms analysis, see pages 60–1.

Soil sample analysis

The soil around the skeleton is being sifted to see if any other personal items were buried with the body. A sample will also be examined in the lab for trace evidence. To find out more about trace evidence, see pages 24–5.

Engraved button

A copper button lies on the skeleton's ribs, and a buckle is found by the pelvis. After quickly cleaning it, CSIs can see the button is engraved with a bird. What can it mean? These items will be taken to a historian who will identify the period they came from.

Cufflink

Sifting the soil, a CSI has found a gold cufflink. It is initialized but years under the soil have made the letters unclear. It will be cleaned with chemicals in the lab to enhance the letters.

Murder weapon?

An old-fashioned pistol has been wrapped in an oilcloth and buried with the body. It is almost certainly the murder weapon, but forensic tests are needed to confirm this. See how such tests are carried out on pages 60–1.

Bones and DNA

The whole skeleton will be taken to the lab and examined by a forensic anthropologist, who will be able to determine the sex and estimate the age of the victim. Turn to pages 58–9 to find out how. If DNA can be extracted, it could confirm the victim's identity. Find out more about DNA on pages 56–7.

FACT FILE

More than 3,000 years after his death, the skeleton of Egyptian pharaoh Tutankhamen was X-rayed. Analysis showed that he did not die of natural causes, as was believed, but had been brutally murdered. The likely assassin succeeded him to the throne.

EVI EVIDENCE

DNA FINGERPRINTING

The discovery of DNA fingerprinting in 1984 changed forensic science forever. Inside the nuclei of the trillions of cells that make up the different parts of our bodies is a map of the features and characteristics that compose individual identity. It was created by a unique combination of our parents' maps. Experts can record this map as a DNA fingerprint—even from a flake of skin left at a crime scene.

Ladder of life

DNA, or deoxyribonucleic acid, is made up of two linked strands that coil around each other like a twisted ladder. The rungs that link the two strands are made of four different chemicals, shown here in different colors. It is the sequence of these chemicals that is different in every person and that forms their DNA fingerprint.

Cloning DNA

Here, an expert carries out a technique called Polymerase Chain Reaction (PCR). When only a fragment of DNA is found, PCR duplicates it until there is a sufficient amount for analysis. PCR works by mimicking the way that DNA copies itself naturally when a cell divides.

Matching DNA

DNA fingerprints are recorded as sequences of rungs, which look similar to a supermarket barcode. Today, crime-scene and offenders' DNA is recorded on national computer databases around the world. The computer software matches thirteen different sequences to find a positive result.

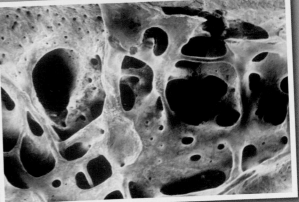

Mothers' DNA

Mitochondrial DNA (mtDNA) is found in a different part of a cell from nuclear DNA. It is inherited only from the mother, so there is little change in it from parent to child. It survives for centuries in bone material (above), and is used to trace female ancestors.

MURDER CASE ANALYSIS

Mitochondrial DNA was extracted from the skeleton found in the rock garden. This is being tested against Mrs. Lawrence, the present owner of Beech House. If she carries the same mtDNA, the skeleton belonged to Jack Macadie, who disappeared in 1918.

MATCH A DNA SAMPLE

Every person has their own unique **DNA** fingerprint. However, much of the information in a **DNA** sequence is the same from person to person. Certain repeating sections are compared in order to find a match.

Which suspect?

Look at the crime-scene sample of DNA shown on the right. Study the possible suspects from the police database, below, and see if you can find a match. To check your answer, go to page 72.

Crime-scene sample

| Suspect 1 | Suspect 2 | Suspect 3 | Suspect 4 |

Twin DNA

DNA analysis has shown that identical twins are just that— exact copies of each other. If a crime was committed by an identical twin, DNA fingerprinting could not identify the guilty one.

FORENSIC ANTHROPOLOGY

Human bodies quickly decompose, leaving only skeletons. When human remains are found, forensic anthropologists get to work. These experts know how to find evidence of identity retained in bones and teeth. If death was violent, they may be able to discover what happened. And if dental records can be traced, experts can discover exactly who inhabited the bones.

The czar's bones

The last Russian czar, Nicholas II, and his family, were believed to have been murdered by Bolshevik forces on the eve of the Russian revolution. In 1998, their skeletons were examined (below) in an attempt to prove the story. Damage to their bones showed that they had indeed been killed in a hail of gunfire.

Talking bones

A human skeleton reveals information about its gender and height in life. Women's pelvises are visibly wider than men's, while three muscle attachment sites on the skull are more prominent in men than in women. Adding around 4 in (10 cm) to the length of a skeleton gives height, but, if the skeleton is incomplete, experts can estimate height by the length of the thighbone or the foot alone.

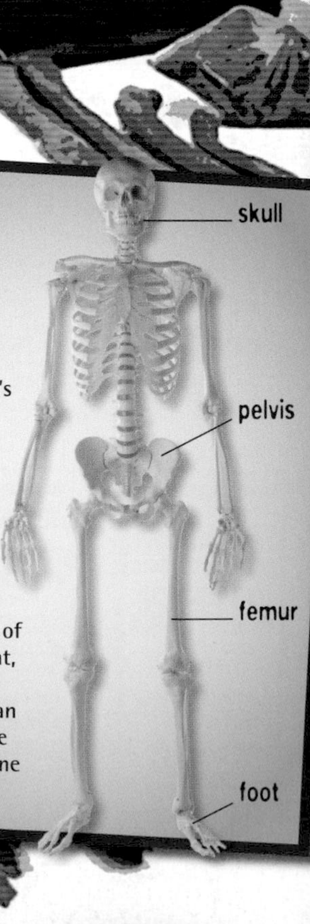

skull

pelvis

femur

foot

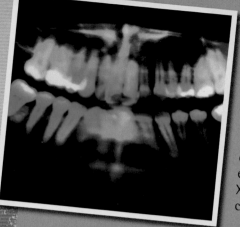

Unique teeth

Dental treatments, such as fillings, are clearly visible under X-ray. And tooth enamel is the hardest substance in the body, so teeth are sometimes the only remains of those killed in explosions and fires. Matching X-rays of teeth to dental records can reliably identify the dead.

MURDER CASE ANALYSIS

A forensic anthropologist is examining the skeleton found at Beech House. She is looking at the size of the pelvis and skull to determine gender, and checking if the collarbone is fully grown. If not, it means the person was under 28 years old.

Growing bones

These X-rays show the hands of a three-year-old and an adult. The child's bones have big gaps between them. Inside the gaps is a tough elastic tissue called cartilage, which is replaced by bone in adulthood. In older people, bones can show signs of deterioration, such as wear and tear on the joints.

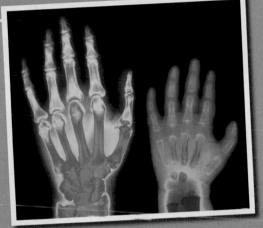

Mongoloid

Negroid

Caucasian

WORK OUT A SUSPECT'S HEIGHT

The length of a grown person's foot is about 15% of their height. If necessary, a forensic anthropologist can estimate height by the bones of the feet alone.

<u>You will need:</u> three adults • a tape measure • a calculator • a pen or pencil • a piece of paper

1. Ask your adults to take off their shoes. Measure their left feet and write the results on your piece of paper next to their names.

2. Now multiply the length of each foot by 7. Write down your results next to the person's name.

3. Measure the adults' heights with your tape measure. How accurate were your results?

Ethnic heads

The skull can be a guide to ethnicity. Mongoloid skulls (Asian origin), have high cheekbones and wide, flat faces; Negroid skulls (Afro-Caribbean origin) are long and narrow with a broad nose cavity; Caucasoid skulls (European origin) are wider than others and have less protruding jaws.

FIREARMS

When a gun is fired, along with a deadly ball of lead it releases a chain of evidence. Tell-tale residue is left on the shooter's hand. The shape and size of the bullet indicates the type of gun it was manufactured for. Tiny markings on the bullet, made by grooves in the gun's barrel, can even lead investigators to the very gun that fired it. Ballistics—a bullet's flight path—can provide valuable evidence too.

Shattered pattern

Finding out how many shots were fired is the firearms investigator's first task. If the bullets have hit reinforced glass, like this car windshield, a clear record is left. The pattern caused by bullet marks in glass can also reveal in which order the shots were fired. Cracks caused by subsequent bullets will not cross over existing cracks.

Ballistics

Laser beams can help investigators discover the flight path of a bullet, showing them exactly where the shooter was standing. The laser is attached to a rod inserted in the bullet hole, and the beam indicates the direction and angle of the bullet's source. The beams can be photographed and produced as evidence in court.

M URDER CASE ANALYSIS

The pistol and bullet from the grave are now at a ballistics lab. An investigator will test-fire the pistol with an unused bullet from the gun's barrel, and then compare markings on the two bullets to confirm that the pistol was the murder weapon.

Brasscatcher

Cartridge cases are as distinctive as the bullets they carry, since the shape of the dent caused by firing varies from gun to gun. The US Brasscatcher database stores images of cartridge cases from guns used in crimes. Cartridge cases collected from a crime scene are compared with those on the database in case a match is found.

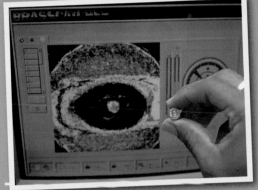

Bullet matching

To match a crime-scene bullet with one from a suspect gun, investigators fire the gun and compare the two bullets. The gun is fired into a water tank so the bullet isn't damaged by impact (as above). Markings on the two bullets are then compared under a comparison microscope.

MATCH A CRIME-SCENE BULLET

When examining bullets, firearms experts look first at the caliber of the bullet. Second, they examine the ridges on the sides of a bullet, known as rifling marks, that are caused by the grooves on the inside of the gun barrel.

Find the bullet fired from the same gun
To match the bullet fired at a crime scene with one fired in the lab, first find a bullet of the correct size, or caliber, then match the rifling marks. To check your answer, turn to page 72.

Crime-scene
bullet

Bullet 1

Bullet 2

Bullet 3

Bullet 4

Bullet 5

Bullet 6

Hand swab

When a gun is fired, the mechanism sprays invisible residues of explosive onto the shooter's hand, which remain for about six hours. When suspects are found at the scene of a shooting, a CSI swabs their hands to collect any gunshot residue. The area between fingers and thumb is most likely to be contaminated.

MURDER
Case Overview

Suspect Profile

Name: Colonel Arthur Macadie

Age in 1918: 55

- Last in line of a respected military dynasty. Won medals of bravery in the Spanish-American War.

- All but disowned his son Jack over his antiwar views.

- Very ill at the time of the disappearance, his doctor did not expect him to live long.

Would the Colonel really murder his own son?

SPRINGFIELD COUNTY POLICE STATION

MISSING PERSON'S REPORT

September 1918

Jack Macadie, a young hero of WWI, was expected home on September 18, 1918, but never arrived. He was discharged on September 8 and was expected at the train station at around 11 o'clock. The stationmaster recalled that a soldier got off the train but could not confirm that it was Private Macadie.

No trace of Jack was found subsequently and the case was closed unsolved.

DNA Report

mtDNA test and Macadie Family Tree

Arthur Macadie (1863–1933)
m.
Lily Hooke (1868–1913)

Elizabeth Macadie (1897–1979) m. Freddie Sarsons (1891–1931)

Jack Macadie (1893–1918) — *the skeleton*

Judith Sarsons (1923–80)

Anne Sarsons (b. 1930)
m.
Bill Lawrence (1926–1999)

The mitochondrial DNA sample taken from the victim's skeleton matched that of Mrs. Anne Lawrence, the present inhabitant of Beech House.

This proves that there is a direct female line between the victim and Anne Lawrence.

The family tree on the left shows that Anne is the daughter of Elizabeth. This means that the skeleton is highly likely to be that of Jack Macadie, Elizabeth's brother.

Trace Evidence Report

Items unearthed next to victim

No significant trace evidence was found by sifting the soil around the skeleton, or through analysis back at the lab.

The items found with the skeleton were examined by a military historian who identified the button and buckle as World War I army issue, identical to those Jack Macadie would have worn as part of his uniform.

A single cufflink was retrieved from the grave, shown on the right in an evidence bag.

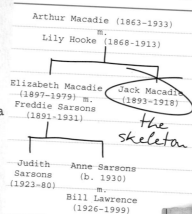

Cufflinks found at scene

Is the first initial J or F?

Local hero airs antiwar opinions!

June 19, 1917

Private Jack Macadie, son of Colonel Arthur Macadie, has spoken about life and death at the Front. He had formerly been missing in action for several months.

"No man should have to endure what I have been through," he told our reporter, gaunt- faced, with one arm in a sling. "The Great War is a mistaken war."

Colonel Macadie has refused to comment on his son's views.

Suspect Profile

Name: Freddie Sarsons
Age in 1918: 27

- A local tailor. Could not enlist for military service due to poor eyesight.
- Cocky, confident type.
- Married Elizabeth while Jack was missing in action. Known locally as a womanizer.
- Widely believed that he expected to inherit Beech House after the Colonel's death.

Who had access to the pistol?

Statement from Mrs. Lawrence

Anne Lawrence knows the family history from her mother:

The Colonel survived until 1933 despite his doctor's diagnosis. He was always tormented by the events preceding Jack's disappearance.

The newlyweds found themselves in financial trouble, even though business was thriving. A balance book found by Mrs. Lawrence shows regular, unexplained withdrawals.

Freddie was shot and killed in a tragic hunting accident in 1931. When the Colonel died two years later, Elizabeth inherited everything.

Ballistics Report

Colt .45 pistol recovered next to victim

Ballistics testing has confirmed that the bullet found in the victim's skull was fired from the gun buried beside the body.

The pistol is a Colt .45 Automatic, a standard issue army pistol. It is engraved with a serial number that has been traced to Colonel Macadie.

Suspect Profile

Name: Elizabeth Macadie
Age in 1918: 21

- Jack's younger sister.
- She was very upset at the rift between Jack and their father.
- She married Freddie Sarsons in 1917 after a whirlwind courtship. They lived in the Macadie family home as Elizabeth was nursing her ailing father.

Suspect Profile

Name: John Farrow
Age in 1918: 59

- The gardener.
- The rock garden where the skeleton was buried was under construction at the time of the disappearance. Farrow had been digging it the morning Jack was due to arrive home.

A modern police trace has found that shortly after the disappearance, he left Beech House, bought his own home in a seaside town, and never worked again.

Why did the gardener leave so abruptly?

Anthropology Report

Examining the bones

Forensic anthropologists have been able to establish that the victim was male, aged over 12 and under 40 years. Bone scarring shows that he had once broken his arm.

Damage to the skull indicates that a gunshot wound to the head was the probable cause of death. The bullet was found inside the skull. The fact that it did not exit the skull suggests that the weapon was fired from a distance.

HISTORY OF FORENSICS

Science has been used to help solve crime since crimes were first committed, but forensic science is more specialized and precise than it has ever been before. Over the last 100 years, major advances have been made in many forensic disciplines, making crime harder than ever to get away with. These advances have also enabled experts to shed light on some historical mysteries, and to solve seemingly impossible cases.

FINGERPRINTING

- In 1856, Sir William Herschel, a British officer in India, began to use thumb prints on documents as a substitute for written signatures for illiterates.

- Before fingerprinting, a system of identification called anthropometry was used by police forces all over the world. It used a complex series of measurements of the body.

- In 1892, Argentina became the first country to replace anthropometry with fingerprints.

- The Federal Bureau of Investigation (FBI) introduced the Automated Fingerprint Identification System (AFIS) in 1975.

- In 1999, the FBI integrated AFIS so that submission, storage, and search could all be carried out electronically using just one system.

Case study

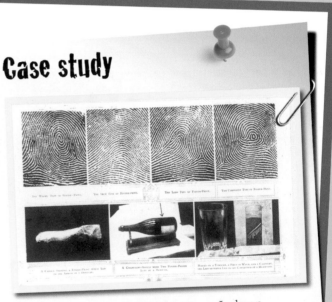

In 1902, 41-year-old burglar Harry Jackson became the first person to be convicted by fingerprint evidence in Britain. After stealing some billiard balls from a London house, Jackson carelessly left his fingerprints on the windowsill. They were photographed and a search of police files of known criminals' prints revealed a match with Jackson, who had just completed a prison term for burglary. The unfortunate burglar was found guilty and sentenced to a harsh seven years in prison. This article (above) from a British newspaper of the same era explains the amazing new technique.

TOXICOLOGY

- In 1813, 26-year-old Spanish doctor Mathieu Orfila published *Treatise of General Toxicology*. Orfila became known as the father of toxicology.

- Before tests for identifying arsenic, it was used so frequently to bump off family members that it became known as "inheritance powder."

- In 1836, British chemist James Marsh first used toxicology in a jury trial, to detect arsenic in a murder victim's body.

- In 1954, R. F. Borkenstein, a police captain in Indiana, invented the Breathalyzer, for detecting alcohol.

Case study

Napoleon I of France died in exile in 1821 and the cause of death was recorded as stomach cancer. But in 1955 the diaries of Napoleon's valet were published, and his description of his master's final months led experts to believe he had in fact been killed by arsenic, given to him in regular doses over a long period. In 2001, a lock of Napoleon's hair was cut into segments and analyzed by toxicologists. The diagnosis was long-term arsenic ingestion.

Case study

On February 14, 1929, in Chicago, seven gang members were gunned down by rival mobsters. The killers left behind 70 cartridge cases, and from these investigators were able to identify the type of machine guns used. Months later, police raided the home of one of the hitmen and seized two guns. An investigator test-fired them and proved them to be the guns used in the St. Valentine's Day Massacre.

FIREARMS

- In 1835, Henry Goddard, one of Scotland Yard's first police officers, used bullet comparison to catch a murderer. He found a visible flaw in the bullet, and traced it back to a mold.

- In 1898, German chemist Paul Jeserich used microphotography to compare the markings on a bullet fired from a suspect's gun to one recovered from the crime scene. The killer was convicted by his evidence.

- The comparison microscope was invented in 1925 in the US by Philip Gravelle and Calvin Goddard, greatly simplifying the comparison of bullets.

DOCUMENTS

- In 1910, American Albert Osborn published *Questioned Documents*, which is still consulted by experts today.

- Two American murderers were convicted in 1924 by forensic evidence proving that a typewriter owned by one of them had been used to type a ransom note.

- British scientists Bob Freeman and Doug Foster invented the electrostatic detection apparatus (ESDA) in 1978.

- In 1998, literary analyst Professor Don Foster helped convict serial bomber Ted Kaczynski by studying documents the killer had composed.

Case study

In 1983, German magazine Stern paid a vast sum for the supposed diaries of Nazi leader Adolf Hitler from the 1930s and '40s. They published the first extracts, and experts and ordinary readers alike furiously debated their authenticity. To end speculation, Stern passed the diaries to forensic experts. They reported that polyester bindings, manufactured in 1953, had been used, and the paper contained a chemical that was not introduced until 1954. Some of the capital letters were different from Hitler's real handwriting. Stern had been swindled.

Case study

In 1995, the world's first DNA database—a collection of DNA fingerprints of suspects and convicted criminals—was begun in Britain. By 2006, the database held profiles for 3.5 million people. Today, DNA databases are a major weapon in the fight against crime all over the world. Advances in searching techniques have made it possible for police to obtain DNA profiles of suspects from past, unsolved crimes, and many cases have been reopened as a result.

DNA

- In 1953, scientists James Watson and Francis Crick discovered the double helix structure of DNA, paving the way for DNA analysis.

- In 1984, British geneticist Alec Jeffries discovered DNA fingerprinting, which uses variations in the genetic code as identification.

- In 1986, Polymerase Chain Reaction (PCR), a method of duplicating parts of a DNA molecule, was developed by scientist Kary Mullis.

- DNA was first used to solve a crime in Britain in 1988. Murderer Colin Pitchfork was convicted using DNA fingerprinting.

TRACE EVIDENCE

- In 1784 in Lancaster, England, John Toms was convicted of murder on the basis of the torn edge of a wad of paper in a pistol matching the remaining piece in his pocket. This was one of the first times physical matching was used to convict.

- Edmund Locard, professor of forensic medicine at the University of Lyons, France, established the first police crime laboratory in 1910. Some ten years later, Locard formulated the basic principle of forensic science: "every contact leaves a trace."

- In 1916, Albert Schneider of California, first used a vacuum apparatus to collect trace evidence.

- The tape lift method of collecting trace evidence was developed in 1950 by Swiss criminalist Max Frei-Sulzer.

- The first high-resolution scanning electron microscopes, used to identify trace evidence, were produced at Cambridge University, England, in 1965.

- In 1977, Masato Soba of Japan first developed latent prints by superglue fuming, a method now commonly used.

Case study

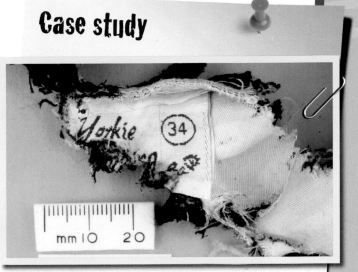

On December 21, 1988, Pan Am Flight 103, flying from London to New York, exploded in midair over the Scottish town of Lockerbie. Examination of the debris revealed that a bomb had caused the explosion, but the investigation failed to progress any further. More than a year later, a passerby found a fragment of gray T-shirt close to the crash site. Incredibly, the blast had left the label intact, enabling detectives to trace the store that had sold the T-shirt. The store owner clearly remembered the purchaser because the man had bought clothes without considering their size or style. With the store owner's description, detectives tracked down the buyer of the T-shirt. They discovered that he had bought it to pack around the bomb.

GLOSSARY

ABO test
A test to determine which of the four major blood groups a sample belongs to.

Accelerant
A substance, such as gasoline, used to make a fire burn more quickly.

Arson
The crime of deliberately starting a fire to cause damage to property.

Ballistics
The science that studies the flight of projectiles. In forensic science it usually refers to bullets.

Bioterrorist
A person who releases deadly poisons, viruses, or bacterium in order to kill and cause panic.

Cartridge case
A tube that contains a bullet and explosive charge for a gun.

Comparison microscope
A double microscope used for viewing two similar items, such as bullets, together, so that a match can be made.

Computer hacker
Someone who uses their computer programming expertise to illegally break into computer systems and change or steal the data there.

Crime scene investigator (CSI)
A person employed by the police to gather forensic evidence at the crime scene.

Database
An organized collection of information on a subject, usually held on computer.

DNA fingerprint
The pattern of repeating sequences in DNA that is unique to each person, and can be used as identification.

Electron microscope
A powerful microscope that uses a stream of electrons to magnify an image.

Electrostatic detection apparatus (ESDA)
A device that can reveal indented writing on paper using static electricity and particles of toner.

Evidence marker
A card for marking the location of key evidence at a crime scene.

Eyewitness
A person who has firsthand knowledge of a crime or other event, because he or she saw it happening.

Fluorescent powder
In forensic science, fluorescent powder is applied to latent fingerprints to make them glow.

Forensic science
Science that is used in an investigation to find evidence linking a suspect to a crime.

Gunshot residue
Microscopic powder sprayed onto the hands of a person firing a gun.

Hard disk
A computer's storage unit. It retains the computer's information when the machine is switched off.

Immunoassay test
A test that determines whether drugs or poisons are present in a sample of blood or urine.

Incendiary
An incendiary fire is one that was started deliberately. In forensics, the word refers to crimes of arson.

Laser beam
A thin intense beam of light used in forensic science to reveal latent fingerprints, and to trace the trajectory of bullets.

Latent fingerprint
One that is not visible and requires special techniques to reveal it.

Literary forensics
A new forensic science that can help identify a suspect by examining the type of language he or she uses in written documents.

Luminol
A chemical spray used by forensic investigators to detect tiny particles of blood. It can even show up years-old traces of blood.

Mass spectrometry
A technique used to discover quantities of drugs present in a sample, and to identify accelerants.

Mitochondrial DNA
DNA found outside the nucleus of some of the body's cells, and containing genetic material passed down from the mother only.

Nuclear DNA
DNA found in the nucleus of cells, and containing an equal amount of genetic material from each parent.

Paramedic
A person trained to give emergency medical treatment.

Polygraph
An instrument for detecting when a suspect is lying, by recording their pulse rate and blood pressure.

Polymerase chain reaction
A method of duplicating fragments of DNA to make a sample large enough for analysis.

Precipitin test
A lab test to establish whether a sample of blood is human.

Presumptive test
A test that determines whether or not a liquid is blood.

Scanner
A device that converts a picture into digital information to be stored on a computer.

Serology
The study of blood and other body fluids, usually to identify a suspect.

Software
Programs that run on a computer, telling it what tasks to perform.

Superglue fuming
A method of revealing latent fingerprints using vapors given off by the glue.

Suspect
Someone who investigators believe is involved in a crime, but who has not been proved guilty.

Toxicology
The study of the nature, effects, and detection of drugs and poisons and the treatment of poisoning.

Trace evidence
Small but measurable amounts of evidence gathered from the crime scene, typically hair, fibers, and soil.

Trajectory
The curving path of a projectile—usually a bullet—through the air.

Ultraviolet light
A light used in forensic science to make fingerprints glow and to detect hidden security features.

X-ray
A type of radiation used to image bones. In forensic science, X-rays are used to make dental identifications.

THE SOLUTIONS

ARSON

ROBBERY

The robbery at the Holbrook Gallery has had police perplexed. Anna Berkhout claims to have been at reception when the painting disappeared, and would have seen anyone entering or leaving the gallery.

The evidence tells us that only two people had traces from the crime scene on their shoes—Ed Kolowski and Jimmy O'Brien. If he had been unconscious before the robbery took place, O'Brien could not have walked on the glass shards. The fingerprints on the lamp stand show that it was he who knocked the security camera away.

He waited until the gallery was empty, put the sedative drug into his own tea, and drank it after having unclipped the painting from its frame. He couldn't have removed the painting from the building, so he must have stashed it in the room, intending to collect it later. Behind one of the other paintings would be the perfect place...

The fire investigator's report concluded that the fire was probably started using gas as an accelerant and a cigar butt to ignite the blaze.

At first glance, Richard Gibbs seems to be the prime suspect. He has a long-running feud with Katherine Holden, the owner of Glad Rags, and the letter received the day before the fire seems to point to him, not to mention the incriminating cigar butt. However, none of the hard evidence points to him. So who has tried to frame Gibbs?

The answer is in the forensics. The muddy footprints left by the door match Karl Caudwell's shoeprint and the indented "L" on the poison pen letter points to his wife, Louise. He could have written the letter on a pad she had previously used, leaving her writing ghosted underneath.

The computer records show that someone had been stealing from the company. Karl was the only person to deal with the accounts. On the night of Katherine's fight with Richard Gibbs, he realized that she was planning to sell up, and that if she did he would be found out. He needed to get rid of the evidence. Using the argument as a cover, he sent the letter to implicate Gibbs. The next night, while his wife was asleep, he returned to the warehouse and started the fire.

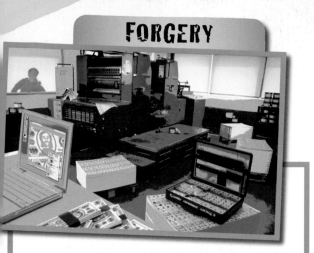

The counterfeiting operation at Night Fly Printers was an ambitious crime. Police found thousands of bills, and it is likely that this is not the first time the forger had been at work at Night Fly. Who had the skills to carry off this crime?

Can it be true that Pete Morelli was unaware of what was happening on his premises? He has the trappings of success while his companies are failing. Is he making his money another way? He was due to board an early morning flight the next day, but he has an alibi for the time the crime took place.

Ray Wallace is a suspicious character, with a track record of fraudulent activity. Is his nervousness caused by guilt, or simply because his criminal record has been revealed? While both his and Pete's fingerprints have been found on the machinery, the eyewitness identified the fleeing suspect as a female.

To catch the criminal, we must turn to the forensic evidence. Who matches the e-fit photo provided by the witness, has blood type A, and left their fingerprints at the scene? The answer is contained in the username that investigators found on the deleted computer files: MONDAY, or Monica Day.

Forensic anthropology and DNA reports identified the skeleton as that of Jack Macadie, who went missing in the fall of 1918.

The missing person's report states that a young soldier was seen getting off a train at the station on the day Jack was due to arrive home. The likelihood is that this was Jack, but he was killed before he ever reached the house.

The pistol found in the grave was traced to Colonel Macadie. Would the shame of Jack's antiwar views have led the Colonel to take the life of his only son? Anyone in the house could have had access to the pistol.

The cufflink found in the grave is the only concrete clue. The initials engraved on it read FS—Freddie Sarsons. The money missing from the family accounts suggests the gardener stumbled on the truth and blackmailed Freddie, explaining his disappearance and subsequent life of comfort.

What could Freddie's motive have been to commit such a terrible crime? With Jack out of the way, and the Colonel very ill, he and Elizabeth would have been in line to inherit the estate. Ultimately though, the plan did not work out. The Colonel lived on despite his illness, so Freddie never received any of his money or the country house. And, in a twist of fate, Freddie himself was shot in a hunting accident 13 years later.

INDEX

ACKNOWLEDGMENTS

Dorling Kindersley would like to thank Precision Printing Ltd. for help with the forgery photoshoot, and Ron Cook for advising on fingerprint patterns.

Index: Hilary Bird
Proofreader: Kitty Nosworthy
Illustrator: Mark Walker

Picture Credits
The publisher would like to thank the following for their kind permission to reproduce their images:

(Key: a=above; b=below/bottom; c=center; f=far; l=left; r=right; t=top)
Academic Press: 35tr. **Alamy Images:** Bloom Works Inc. 4, 6; Simon Clay 46c; Ilene MacDonald 57br; SHOUT 49tl; Stock Connection 47c; Jack Sullivan 23cr; Phil Talbot 34tl. **Camera Press:** Gamma 11tl. **Corbis:** Nogues Alain 34bl; Archivo Iconografico, S.A. 65tr; Bettmann 66t; Andrew Brookes 23tl, 57tl; L. Clarke 24bl; Richard Hamilton

Smith 6bl; Brownie Harris 36–37c; Ed Kashi 19tl, 19br; Thom Lang 6t; Reuters 23br; Tom Salyer 45cr; Joseph Sohm 9tr; Bill Stormont 32c; Zefa 2–3, 18, 27cra. **DK Images:** The British Museum 44cr. **ECB:** 44cb. **Empics Ltd:** AP 58; AP / Elise Amendola 33tr; AP/Douglas C. Pizac 60r; John Giles 9c; Mike Hutmacher 32cr; PA Photos 13tl, 67; Chris Parkiap 11cl; Chris Young 12. **Picture courtesy of Foster & Freeman Ltd:** 37bl, 37bc, 45cla. **Getty Images:** Peter Dawson 11br; Sam Diephuis 34c; Hulton Archive 63bl; Fernando Laszlo 59bc; Steve Liss 61t, 61c. **Mary Evans Picture Library:** 64. **Esther Neate** (www.neateimaging.com): 49c, 49cl. **popperfoto. com:** 10–11c. **Reuters:** Viktor Korotayev 60l. **Rex Features:** Lehtikuva Oy 44clb; Sonny Meddle 55fcr, 71cr; MGG 11cra; Sipa Press 9tl. **The Ronald Grant Archive:** 65b. **Science Photo Library:** 21tl, 24cb, 48bc, 59tl, 59c; Dr. Jeremy Burgess 25tr; Michael Donne 11tr; Mauro Fermariello 13cr, 21br, 25tl, 49cra, 61br; Spencer Grant 13cl; Steve Gschmeissner 24cr; Insolite Realite 57tr; James

King–Holmes 21cl; Robert Longuehaye, NIBSC 56b; Jerry Mason 46bl; Alfred Pasieka 20br; Philippe Psaila 44bc; Sandia National Laboratories 19cr; Dr. Jurgen Scriba 22; Tek Image 9bl, 66b; Sheila Terry 35tl; Geoff Tompkinson 23tr; Michel Viard/ Peter Arnold Inc. 25cr. **TopFoto.co.uk:** 45tl.

All other images © Dorling Kindersley
For further information see: www.dkimages.com

Solutions to the activities
Page 45 The authentic identity card is the one belonging to Mary Lynham. There are five mistakes on Juan Castalino's card: the hologram is wrong; the card number is too short; the issue date is nonexistent; "last name" is spelled incorrectly; the stamp over the photograph is missing.
Page 57 Suspect 2.
Page 61 Bullet 3.